DEC 1 1998

50

WITHDRAWN
from
Osterville Village Library

OSTERVILLE FREE LIBRARY
43 WIANNO AVE.
OSTERVILLE, MA 02655
(508) 428-5757

EARLY AMERICAN FAMILY

Meet the Drakes
on the Kentucky Frontier

by John J. Loeper

WITHDRAWN
from
Osterville Village Library

OSTERVILLE FREE LIBRARY
43 WIANNO AVE.
OSTERVILLE, MA 02655
(508) 428-5757

BENCHMARK BOOKS

MARSHALL CAVENDISH
NEW YORK

Benchmark Books
Marshall Cavendish Corporation
99 White Plains Road
Tarrytown, New York 10591-9001

Text copyright ©1999 by John J. Loeper
Illustrations copyright © 1999 by Marshall Cavendish Corporation
All rights reserved

Illustrations by James Watling
Musical score and arrangement by Jerry Silverman
Map by Rodica Prato
Photo research by Matthew J. Dudley

The photographs in this book are used by permission and through the
courtesy of: *Raymond Bial*: 10, 16, 23, 25, 26, 31, 33, 34, 43, 48, 58, back cover.
The Image Bank/Peter Beney: 8. *Courtesy Jonesborough-Washington County History
Museum*: 39. *Photo Taken at Museum of Appalachia, Norris, Tennessee/photo by
Don Dudenbostel*: 50.

Library of Congress Cataloging-in-Publication Data
Loeper, John J.
Meet the Drakes on the Kentucky frontier / John J. Loeper.
p. cm. — (Early American family)
Includes bibliographical references and index.
Summary: Chronicles the emigration of the Drake family from Virginia to the
Kentucky wilderness in 1788, their settlement, home construction, daily chores,
education, food, entertainment, and social activities.
ISBN 0-7614-0845-2 (lib. bdg.)
1. Pioneers—Kentucky—Social life and customs—Juvenile literature.
2. Pioneers—Kentucky—Biography—Juvenile literature. 3. Kentucky—Social life
and customs—Juvenile literature. 4. Frontier and pioneer life—Kentucky—
Juvenile literature. 5. Drake family—Juvenile literature. [1. Drake family.
2. Pioneers. 3. Kentucky—Social life and customs. 4. Frontier and pioneer life—
Kentucky.] I. Title. II. Series: Loeper, John J.
Early American family.
F455.L76 1999   976.9—DC21   97-42198   CIP   AC

Printed in Hong Kong
1 3 5 6 4 2

To the Reader

During the early years of our country's history, restless Americans moved out from the original thirteen colonies to explore and settle the lands east of the Mississippi River. This was America's first frontier.

America was a vast country, largely unexplored. Early hunters and trappers returned with exciting stories of faraway places. There were endless tracts of land, huge forests, abundant water, and a rich store of game. Farmers back east heard these tales and believed them. They sold their possessions and headed west, led by ambition, a thirst for adventure, and the lure of cheap land. It was said that two dollars could buy a hundred acres on the frontier.

After the Revolution, America spread to the Mississippi. Following the Louisiana Purchase in 1803, her boundaries seemed endless. The nation was growing in size and number. A population of just over a million and a half in 1760 had grown to four million by 1790.

Americans found plenty of open space, but it was often wild and desolate. Families were on their own. They built their own houses, grew their own food, supplied their own medicine, and provided their own entertainment. They had few neighbors and had to work hard with few distractions. Yet they created a life for themselves.

This is the story of a real family. The Drakes settled in southeastern Kentucky near the Kentucky River. The year was 1788. Seven years earlier, in 1781, the British had surrendered at Yorktown. One year later, in 1789, George Washington became the first president of the United States. It was a time of new beginnings, when the Drake family set out for the Kentucky frontier.

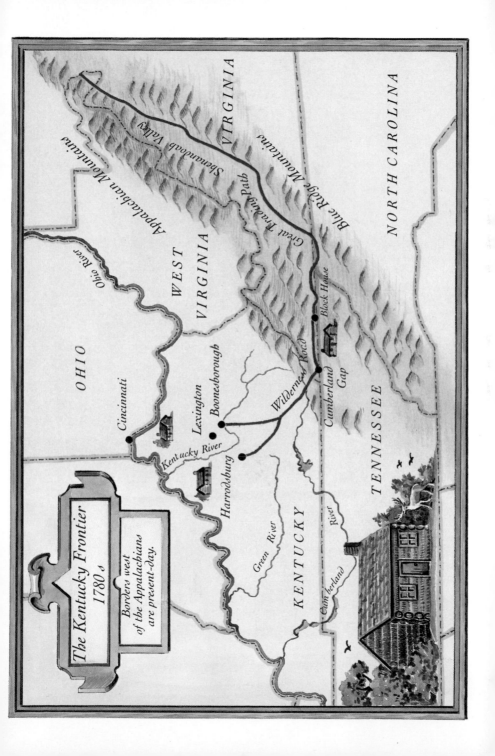

The Kentucky Frontier
1780s

Borders west
of the Appalachians
are present-day.

OHIO

Ohio River

Cincinnati

WEST VIRGINIA

Lexington

Boonesborough

Kentucky River

Harrodsburg

Green River

KENTUCKY

Cumberland River

Wilderness Road

Cumberland Gap

Black House

Great Trading Path

Shenandoah Valley

Appalachian Mountains

VIRGINIA

Blue Ridge Mountains

NORTH CAROLINA

TENNESSEE

One morning, Isaac Drake, a Virginia farmer, looked out of his bedroom window at a cloudless sky. It was springtime, and the fields and woodlands were brushed with green. Apple and peach trees were lush with blossoms. The Shenandoah Valley was at its best.

Off in the distance Isaac saw the hazy outline of the Blue Ridge Mountains. They ringed the valley. He wondered what lay beyond them. His inborn curiosity had brought his family from New Jersey to Pennsylvania and on to Virginia. One thing was certain—there was plenty of room in this new country and no need to stay in one place.

A writer of the period observed with humor: "People scarcely squatted down in one place,

Off in the distance Isaac saw the hazy outline of the Blue Ridge Mountains.

than they hear of another where corn grows without planting and cotton comes already picked and baled, so they pull up stakes and move on until they hear something better."

"The curse of our country is too much land," a politician complained. "People refuse to stay put!"

While Isaac Drake watched the sun rise slowly over those faraway mountains, he felt the familiar urge to move on. He had heard wonderful stories about the frontier. He was itching to go there and see for himself.

In a room behind the kitchen, the three Drake boys, Dan, Benjamin, and Jonathan, woke to another day of farmwork. They climbed out of their beds, stretched, and rubbed the sleep from their eyes. Then they washed their faces with cold water from a bucket and dressed. Dan was the first one ready. His brothers teased him by calling him "Farmer Dan." He liked to tend the animals and work in the fields. Ben and Jonathan, on the other hand, would have preferred to stay in bed.

The boys heard their mother singing in the kitchen while she prepared breakfast. Breakfast was a hearty meal. Today, their mother was making a big dish of hoecakes. Made of cornmeal and water, these pancakes were a common sight on kitchen tables. They were called hoecakes because, in earlier times, they had been baked over campfires on the blade of a hoe.

Today, their mother was making a big dish of hoecakes.

Hoecakes

2 cups cornmeal   1 cup boiling water
1/2 teaspoon salt   butter

Combine the cornmeal and salt. Stir in water and
let cool. Shape portions into small patties and fry on
a well-greased griddle, browning on both sides. Serve
with butter and syrup.

While the family ate, the boys were assigned
their daily chores. The farm was not a large one
but it required constant attention. There were
fences to mend and cows to milk. Even six-year-
old Jonathan helped out by collecting kindling
for the fire and feeding the chickens.

Before breakfast was over, Mr. Drake brought
up the subject of the land beyond the mountains.

"They say it's a wonderland. One man told
me there's no winter. Crops grow year-round.
Think of it, fresh vegetables in January!"

"Sounds like a lot more work. A body needs
winter to rest up," Lizzy Drake told him. Then
she looked at her husband with suspicion.

The farm was not a large one but it required
constant attention.

"Are you thinking of moving on?" she asked.

"The idea has crossed my mind," he admitted.

"We have very little money," Mrs. Drake cautioned.

"They tell me that the land beyond the mountains is cheap. Some of it is free, there for the taking."

"It sounds too good to be true!" Mrs. Drake exclaimed.

"That's not so," her husband protested. "It's unsettled land out there in Kentucky and Ohio."

"They're not yet states. It's Indian territory," Mrs. Drake countered. "And what about this place?"

"We could sell this place, pay our debts, and have a tidy sum remaining."

The boys listened attentively to their parents' exchange. With the exception of Dan, the brothers seemed excited about the notion of a new home.

"I would have to leave school," Dan said, sadly.

He was ten years old and attended a school in the valley. It had only a dozen pupils, but Dan knew how to read and write and add and subtract. Benjamin, who was eight, went to school, too, but was less attentive to his lessons.

"I'm afraid there will be no school in the wilderness, Dan. But that's not important. You are going to be a farmer, and farm folks don't need much schooling."

Dan lowered his head and said nothing. Despite what his brothers called him, he did not want to be a farmer. He had another dream. Someday he hoped to read about history and science and faraway places. Learning new things not only excited him but aroused his curiosity to learn more. But for now, he had to do what he was told.

After a few weeks of pressing the matter, Mr. Drake had convinced his wife to move on. The farm was put up for sale, and the family began to prepare for the journey.

Ownership of the Mississippi River and the land that lay west of the thirteen colonies was in dispute. There were claims and counterclaims. Connecticut and Massachusetts demanded northern sections, while New York and Georgia wanted lands to the south. While the disagreements raged, people continued to settle the frontier.

An area of particular interest was a place called *Kentahthe* by the Cherokee, meaning "land of tomorrow." It was a land that had been explored by frontiersmen such as Daniel Boone. They came back filled with images of this "blue-grass" country, so called for the blue-green grass that grew there, and stories of a wild, open land.

It was a place where dreams might come true.

Kentucky was a place where dreams might come true.

"Kentucky is the promised land, the land of milk and honey," proclaimed a newspaper of the period.

Many of the first settlers came from Virginia. Later, people arrived from New Jersey, Maryland, and Pennsylvania. The total population of Kentucky, which numbered only a few hundred in 1780, would reach close to seventy-five thousand by 1790.

Many years later, Dan wrote in his diary:

When we first arrived there were few inhabitants. Within six years the number of settlers had increased so that one could not wander a mile in any direction without coming upon another cabin.

The way to Kentucky was not easy. The Drakes retraced the route of Daniel Boone through the mountains and followed Indian trails through the forests. Kentucky was a natural extension of Virginia. No land survey determined where Virginia left off and Kentucky began. Only the stony face of the Appalachian Mountains set the two regions apart. The steep rock walls of

The Drakes retraced the route of Daniel Boone through the mountains and followed Indian trails through the forests.

the mountains formed a natural barrier between them. The Drakes passed through a gap in these walls, which led them into a maze of valleys in what is now eastern Kentucky. This was the Cumberland Gap, a mountain doorway to the western frontier.

A song from the time paints a colorful picture of the Cumberland Gap and the rough-and-tumble ways on the frontier:

The first white man in Cumberland Gap,
The first white man in Cumberland Gap,
The first white man in Cumberland Gap,
Was Doctor Walker, an English chap.

Daniel Boone on Pinnacle Rock,
(repeat two times)
He killed Indians with an old flintlock.

Cumberland Gap with its cliff and rocks,
(repeat two times)
Home of the panther, bear, and fox.

Me and my wife and my wife's grand'pap,
(repeat two times)
All raise Hell in Cumberland Gap.

I've got a woman in Cumberland Gap,
(repeat two times)
She's got a boy that calls me "pap."

In the summer of 1788, after months of arduous travel, a wagon drawn by two horses tossed and tumbled over the rocky surface of southeastern Kentucky. A hound dog trudged along behind it, ears flapping with every step. His name was Old Lion, and he had been with the

Drakes since he was a pup. Dan had found him in the fields, a stray, most likely born in the woods. When they saw him, Ben and Jonathan laughed. They said he was scrawny and good for nothing. But Dan took the sad-eyed pup under his wing and named it Old Lion.

As the sun was setting, the dog ran ahead, sniffing the unfamiliar ground. The horses, catching up to him, came to a halt. The wagon had reached a wide clearing with a stream running through it.

"This is it!" Mr. Drake shouted. "This is the place we've been looking for!" His wife and sons jumped off the wagon and looked around. They saw nothing but wilderness. Surely their father was joking? But he was already unpacking the wagon—out came axes, knives, rifles, skillets, kettles, and blankets. Dan and his father quickly set up a lean-to using tree branches and canvas. While their mother gathered fixings for a meal, Jonathan collected wood, and Ben started a fire. The Drake family was settling in.

"Is this where we are going to live, Ma?" Jonathan asked.

The wagon had reached a wide clearing with a stream running through it.

"I sure hope so," Lizzy Drake answered. "Your Pa is a natural wanderer. He's always hankering for someplace new. I sure hope this spot will do and we can stay put."

She thought back to those days on the Virginia farm. She was happy there. She had made a good home for her family. Now she had to start all over again. A sadness overcame her, and she brushed away a tear from her eye.

"Ma is feeling sad," Jonathan whispered to Ben. "I think she wants to go back home to Virginia."

"That's not home anymore," Ben reminded his little brother, throwing an arm over his shoulder. "This is our home now."

"Hurry, you boys," Lizzy Drake chided her sons. "Stop chattering! We have work to do!"

During the next few weeks the boys helped their father clear a small plot of land. The woods were cut back. As axes were heaved in battle against the wilderness, a cabin rose log by log. Felled trees were trimmed and the logs notched and fitted together. Mr. Drake laid a plank roof

As axes were heaved in battle against the wilderness, a cabin rose log by log.

and sawed an opening in the wall for a window. The boys covered the hole with a translucent animal skin and hung a plank door with rawhide hinges. All the woodwork was done by hand, using an axe or a saw. Finally, a fireplace and chimney were fashioned out of stone held together with a mud mortar.

The interior of the cabin was as plain and

WITHDRAWN
from
Osterville Village Library

OSTERVILLE FREE LIBRARY

The interior of the cabin was as plain and simple as its construction.

simple as its construction. The dirt floor was covered with dried grass. Mr. Drake put together a few pieces of furniture on the spot. A slab from a tree trunk laid on top of four legs, quickly split from a log, served as a table. Benches were made from sawed-off planks left over from the roofing. Beds were mounds of dry leaves covered with a blanket. A few pegs driven into the wall held the family clothing.

Moving into the cabin was a simple matter.

The few possessions brought from Virginia were easy to put away. They were mostly utensils for the kitchen and tableware. With plenty of firewood stacked outside the door and enough game to ward off hunger, the Drake family was settled in before the first snow of the winter.

The winter of 1788 was one of the harshest in memory. There were heavy snows and intense cold. Sheets of ice blocked eastern harbors, and snow piled up in the mountain passes.

In the Drakes' cabin, not even the roaring fire and the thick quilts brought from Virginia could keep out the cold. Many nights the three boys huddled together to keep warm. Even Old Lion was invited to their mattress of dried leaves.

Throughout that winter their father's rifle kept the cooking pots full of game. The family ate squirrel, rabbit, raccoon, and venison. They drank water from melted snow and made hoecakes and mush from cornmeal.

It was a hard season with long, cold nights. Dan often took Old Lion out for a run in the moonlight. The stars were brilliant overhead.

Dan often took Old Lion out for a run in the moonlight.

When Dan looked up at them they reminded him of all the things he wanted to know about the world. *Someday,* he promised himself, *I will learn about the heavens and the earth.*

Winter days melted into spring. Almost overnight, the Kentucky landscape became tinged with green and carpets of violets. Robins and tiny yellow finches fluttered in the treetops.

With a good measure of luck and frontier hardiness, the Drake family survived the winter without illness. It was time then to start the hard work of establishing a farm in the wilderness. Land had to be cleared for a cornfield. Lizzy Drake planted a vegetable garden, and she and the boys gathered wild fruits and nuts.

There was very little free time during that first year. Yet, as the years passed, the Drake farm grew and prospered. Livestock was obtained by bartering with distant neighbors. Lizzy swapped one of her skillets for a rooster and a few hens, and two bags of dried corn were exchanged for the pigs. By the third year, the family owned a cow, two sheep, two pigs, and a flock of chickens.

Lizzie Drake planted a vegetable garden.

For the Drake boys, life on the frontier was demanding. They helped their father in the fields and around the farm. Dan watered and fed the livestock. Ben split logs for fences, and Jonathan stacked firewood. In a home without girls, the boys had to help their mother too. They swept the floor, washed clothes, and spun wool. Most of the family's staples—meat, dairy products, vegetables, and flour—were produced and processed at home. Meat was smoked and dried; milk was churned into butter; and wheat was ground in a crude mill.

Mrs. Drake had many responsibilities. It seemed her work was never done! She not only prepared meals, she also made clothing. She fashioned jackets and moccasins out of deerskin. She scraped and stitched hides and knitted caps and stockings. She was also a candle maker, a soap maker, and the family doctor, scouring the woods for herbs and barks to use as medicine. Tea made from sassafras bark was her cure for a fever, and peppermint tea soothed a sore stomach.

Mr. Drake was a good shot, and the animals that he killed with his rifle on hunting trips in the forest provided the family with much more than food. Deer not only provided meat, but

The boys swept the floor, washed clothes, and spun wool.

The animals that Mr. Drake killed with his rifle on hunting trips in the forest provided the family with much more than food.

the pelts were turned into jackets, trousers, and moccasins. The antlers were carved into combs and buttons. Bearskins made blankets and floor coverings. Soap came from animal fat, and candles were shaped from beeswax. From the forest, too, came wood—which was in constant demand for cooking and heating as well as for the furniture and tools that were fashioned during the long winter months. On the frontier most everything necessary for daily life came from nature.

Even entertainment was found outdoors. The boys played hide-and-seek among the cornstalks. They sailed boats made from acorn caps along the stream. They skipped pebbles across the pond. Old Lion flushed out rabbits and squirrels from the underbrush, which the boys pretended to hunt with play rifles made from tree branches.

One of their favorite pastimes was to sit on the ground in a circle and play what they called their "Guess What?" game. Dan, being the oldest and the best with words, would stump his brothers by making up riddles. He'd keep them guessing for hours before revealing the answer.

> *What did the ocean say to Noah in his ark?*
> *(It didn't say anything. It just waved.)*
>
> *What did the field say when it began to rain?*
> *(If this keeps up, my name will be mud.)*
>
> *What did the dog say when he lost his tail?*
> *(It won't be long now.)*
>
> *Why does a pigeon roost on one leg?*
> *(Because if he lifted it he would fall down.)*

Although life on the frontier was busy, it was often lonesome. Neighbors were miles away. In the beginning there were neither churches nor schools. The loneliness of their lives made frontier folk welcome any visitor. A passing hunter, a neighbor on the way to a distant mill, or a peddler with a wagon full of wonders were always asked to stay. The peddler was especially welcome, since he also brought news of a new family down the way or what fashionable city people were wearing. An old lyric describes the peddler's stock in trade:

Pins and needles, pots and pans,
baskets, washbowls, crocks, and cans,
whistles, kettles for boil or stew,
china figures, old or new
spectacles and nutmeg graters,
and platters for your fish and taters.
He's full of news and a frequent lie,
told in jest to make you buy.

Circuit riders were also welcome guests. These men were traveling ministers willing to endure a life on horseback and many nights sleeping on the ground. With Bibles in their saddlebags and the Lord's words ever-ready, they felt that God had called them to preach. They ranged over a huge territory, bringing words of hope to the lonely settlers scattered throughout the frontier. They crossed mountain passes, forded rivers, and braved storms of wind and snow. They preached to households by fire-light and helped organize congregations of the faithful. One circuit rider, a Methodist named Peter Cartwright, traveled the frontier over a fifty-year period, preaching over 14,000 sermons.

Camp meetings were the best way of gathering

people together. A suitable site was chosen, and the circuit rider spread the word that a meeting was scheduled. People came by foot, on horseback, and in wagons to hear the preaching. But camp meetings were also the perfect excuse to have some fun. People got together to meet old friends and to make new ones. Between sermons, the camp was abuzz with talk about politics and the going price for corn and barley. Often the camp meeting resulted in the formation of a congregation and the building of a church.

At one of the camp meetings, Benjamin, who had just turned thirteen, met a pretty, quick-witted girl from a nearby farm. Her name was Helen, and she won Ben's heart. Three years later, he would be the first of the Drake boys to marry.

The early settlers on the frontier generally married young. Sixteen was considered a marriageable age. It was easy enough to set up another household. The settlers would simply join together to put up another cabin, just as they would pitch in to build the church where Helen and Benjamin were married.

The first schools on the frontier grew out of these churches. "Know the truth and the truth shall set you free" was a favorite biblical quote of the circuit riders. But to know the truth, one had to be able to read the Bible. Children needed lessons in reading if they were to become good church members.

"Brothers and Sisters, hear me," the circuit rider preached. "You must teach your children to read the Good Book. This is you duty. And

Children needed lessons in reading if they were to become good church members.

At one of the camp meetings, Benjamin, who had just turned thirteen, met a pretty, quick-witted girl from a nearby farm.

if you can't teach your children, then you must find someone who can."

Many of the settlers weren't very good readers themselves. So, the Drakes and a dozen other families got together and decided to build a schoolhouse and hire a teacher. Dan was delighted when he heard the news. His brothers were less enthusiastic.

"Maybe we won't have to go to school," Jonathan speculated one day.

"Don't you want to learn things?" Dan questioned.

"I don't need to learn things, I know everything now!"

Dan and Benjamin laughed. "Do you know how many inches there are in a foot?" Dan asked.

"'Course I do," Jonathan said. "As many inches as it takes to make a foot!"

"How many is that?" Ben teased.

"That's for me to know and for you to find out," Jonathan replied.

The school building was a rough one-room log cabin. It was fitted with crude benches and

The school building was a rough one-room log cabin.

long tables. There were open windows at both ends to let in daylight, and a fireplace against one wall provided minimal heat in winter.

One of the circuit riders was hired as the teacher with the understanding that he could board at the various cabins the school served.

His first discharge of duty was to post a list of rules:

> *Pupils are to appear at the Schoolhouse each morning by half an hour after sunrise; with hands and faces cleanly washed and hair neatly combed. There is to be no teasing, laughing, whispering, fighting, swearing or lying. Those who disobey will be subject to the rod.*

A typical school day began early and ended late. Children often arrived home after sunset. Attendance was not compulsory, and both boys and girls were welcome to join the class. Children of all ages huddled together in overcrowded one-room schoolhouses doing lessons largely by rote. Learning was often a struggle. "It's little they pays me," a frontier teacher said, "and little I teaches 'em."

Children were taught the basics—reading, writing, and arithmetic. Numbers were needed on a farm. There were eggs to count, vegetables to weigh, and measurements to take. Dan and some of the older students learned such things as the names of the planets and the plants that grew in the forest.

"Read to me from Leviticus, Dan," Mrs. Drake asked one evening. Pulling a lighted candle to an open Bible, young Dan began to read.

"Pay attention boys!" Mr. Drake scolded Ben and Jonathan, who were playing with Old Lion. "Your brother is reading from the Good Book."

Following the words with his finger, Dan read aloud. ". . . I will walk among you and be your God, and you shall be my people."

"Amen!" Mr. Drake exclaimed.

"It's good that Dan can go back to his learning," Mrs. Drake said with a sidelong look at her husband.

"I suppose every family should have one person who knows something other than farming," said Mr. Drake.

A wide grin crossed Dan's face. Perhaps he would not have to be a farmer after all!

A special treat came once a year in the late spring. The entire family looked forward to it. This was the trip to the country store in a village twenty miles away. Early that morning the wagon was hitched and loaded with hides and

Following the words with his finger, Dan read aloud.

pelts collected throughout the winter. These would be traded for salt, spices, coffee, tea, pencils, glasses, and whatever else was needed. At a country store one could buy most anything, from sugar to wallpaper. Mrs. Drake would concentrate on the stock of gloves and bonnets. Mr. Drake might trade a pelt for a few Spanish

At a country store one could buy almost anything, from sugar to wallpaper.

cigars. The boys made their way straight to the candy counter and its store of chocolate, molasses taffy, and licorice.

Over the years, as the Drake farm prospered, their cabin expanded. An extra room was added, and a plank floor was laid. The population of Kentucky was growing too. Lexington, fifty miles away and the chief commercial center of the frontier, now had almost two thousand residents. It published its own newspaper and had built a library in the center of town.

The Lexington library played a part in shaping Dan's life. One of his teachers borrowed a science book for Dan to read. It had a section on human anatomy. Soon he was able to name all the bones in the body.

One day, when Dan was seventeen, he asked his father for permission to apprentice to a doctor. In those times, medicine was learned by working alongside a practicing physician. The apprentice lived with the doctor and learned from him.

At first, Mr. Drake objected.

"You are the oldest boy and you belong on

Over the years, as the Drake farm prospered, their cabin expanded.

the farm," he told him. "You can't earn a proper living peddling pills and powders."

At the time, doctors did not enjoy the prestige they do today. The practice of medicine was unregulated, and success was uncertain. Most people mistrusted doctors and relied on home remedies instead.

Dan was crushed.

"If that is what you want, keep on hoping," his mother encouraged. "Someday your Pa may change his mind."

On Dan's eighteenth birthday, he and Jonathan were helping their father in the field. They stopped to rest for a moment, and Isaac Drake announced that he had a birthday surprise for Dan.

"I've talked with the preacher," he told him. "He knows a doctor in Cincinnati who will take you on as an apprentice."

Dan could hardly believe what he heard.

"We will have to go to Ohio to see him and make all the arrangements," his father continued.

Dan threw his arms around his father's waist and hugged him. "Thank you, Pa!" he said.

Weeks later, Dan and his father set off for Cincinnati. He kissed his mother goodbye and whispered in her ear.

"Thanks, Ma. I know you had something to do with this," he said.

His mother just smiled.

"Learn all you can and become a good doctor," she called after him as the family wagon pulled away.

Later that year, Benjamin and Helen were married and started a family of their own in a new cabin at the edge of the farm. Three years later, Jonathan married a girl from South Fork and built a cabin nearby. The two boys stayed on the farm with their father. And Lizzy Drake was happy again. She had made a new home. Her boys were grown, and she knew she was here to stay.

To most of us today, a family's moving to a strange and lonely place might seem to show a lack of common sense. Yet this was the spirit of the time. People were willing, even anxious, to conquer the wilderness and survive. The lack

"Learn all you can and become a good doctor," Lizzy called after Dan as the family wagon pulled away.

of proper schools simply meant that learning was acquired in other ways. With or without a church, religion survived.

This frontier spirit has found its way into our daily language. We get "mad as a hornet" and can be "stubborn as a mule." People still "jump down your throat." But there is one saying that sums up the spirit of the frontier:

> Do what you can and what you get hold,
> Belief in yourself is better than gold.

This is what the Drake family did. And when Kentucky became a state in 1792, the Drakes were among its first families.

Many years later, after becoming a prominent doctor and a teacher of medicine, Dan wrote:

> If I were to write a recipe for making great and good men and women, I would have the family placed in the woods, given simple food, dressed in plain clothes, and made to join in rural work and pleasure.

The Drake Family Tree

The Drake family originated in Great Britain. Drakes came to America and settled in New Jersey around 1690. There are more than 85,000 Drakes in the United States today.

Due to inaccurate record keeping, the following dates are approximate.

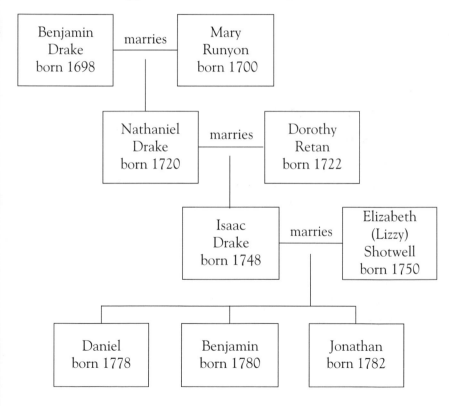

Places to Visit

To find out more about how people lived on the first frontier, you can visit these historic sites:

Cannonsburgh, Murfreesboro, Tennessee
This re-created village, including a grist mill, a frontier church, and an early log structure called the Leeman House, depicts pioneer life.

Cumberland Gap National Historical Park, Middlesboro, Kentucky
Hensley Settlement, a reconstructed frontier village, is found here at the starting point of the Wilderness Road.

Frontier cabin, Kentucky

Jonesboro Historic District, Jonesboro, Tennessee
Chartered in 1799, Jonesboro, with its many
historic buildings, is the oldest town in the state.

Levi Jackson Wilderness Road State Park, London,
Kentucky
Mountain Life Museum, which is found in the park,
has rustic cabins with split-rail fences.

Old Washington, Washington, Kentucky
Founded in 1784, Washington was the second-
largest town in Kentucky, with 119 log cabins.
Thirty-five sites and seven historic buildings are
open to the public.

Books to Read

To learn more about life on the American frontier, here are some books you might enjoy:

Nonfiction

Anderson, Joan W. *Pioneer Children of Appalachia.* New York: Houghton Mifflin, 1990.

Clark, Thomas D. *Simon Kenton, Kentucky Scout.* Ashland, KY: Jesse Stuart Foundation, 1993.

Fisher, Leonard E. *Colonial Craftsmen: The Doctors.* Tarrytown, NY: Marshall Cavendish, 1997.

Greenberg, Judith E. and Helen C. McKeever. *A Pioneer Woman's Memoir.* Danbury, CT: Franklin Watts, 1995.

Sanford, William R. and Carl R. Green. *Daniel Boone: Wilderness Pioneer.* Springfield, NJ: Enlow, 1997.

Smith, Adam and Katherine S. Smith. *A Historical Album of Kentucky.* Brookfield, CT: The Millbrook Press, 1995.

Fiction

Altsheler, Joseph A. *Kentucky Frontiersmen: The Adventures of Henry Ware, Hunter and Border Fighter.* Williamstown, MA: Voyageur Publishing, 1988.

Chamber, Catherine E. *Daniel Boone and the Wilderness Road.* Mahwah, NJ: Troll Publications, 1984.

———. *Log Cabin Home: Pioneers in the Wilderness.* Mahwah, NJ: Troll Publications, 1984.

Fritz, Jean. *The Cabin Faced West.* New York: Putnam, 1987.

Henry, Joanne. *Log Cabin in the Woods: A True Story About a Pioneer Boy.* New York: Four Winds Press, 1988.

Luttrell, Wanda. *Home on Stoney Creek.* Colorado Springs, CO: Chariot Family, 1994.

———. *Reunion in Kentucky.* Colorado Springs, CO: Chariot Family, 1994.

Index

Page numbers for illustrations are in **boldface**.

About the Author

J. Loeper was born in Ashland, Pennsylvania. He has been a teacher, counselor, and school administrator. He has both taught and studied in Europe.

Mr. Loeper has contributed articles and poems to newspapers, journals, and national magazines. He is the author of more than a dozen books for young readers, all dealing with American history, and an active member of several historical societies. The *Chicago Sun* called him the "young reader's expert on Americana."

Mr. Loeper is also an exhibiting artist and has illustrated one of the books he authored. He and his wife divide their time between Connecticut and Florida.